Eidotheosophy
God Supports
The 4B Movement

Vanida Plamondon

EIDOTHEOSOPHY - GOD SUPPORTS THE 4B MOVEMENT

First edition. November 16, 2024.

ISBN: 979-8230743873

Written by Vanida Plamondon.

The 4B Movement

The 4B movement is about reclaiming autonomy and establishing a personal stand for respect and dignity. This movement's name represents a choice to refrain from four traditional expectations often placed on women: dating men, getting married, having sex with men, and having children. For many women, these decisions reflect a way to resist systems that, intentionally or not, strip away their control and turn their choices into social or economic obligations. In a world that has often dictated what women should do with their bodies, hearts, and time, the 4B movement emerges as a radical, yet deeply personal, refusal to conform to those pressures. Instead, it's a movement built on the belief that unless a woman has full agency over these core aspects of her life, she should feel free, and even spiritually called, to choose herself over society's expectations.

When we talk about the 4B movement, we're not just talking about personal choices that women might make on a whim. These decisions go to the heart of how women's lives have been structured and controlled. So often, marriage, motherhood, and even dating have been treated as inevitable milestones for women. Many societies make it seem like a woman's value is defined by her relationship status or her willingness to bear children. And while these relationships and roles can be fulfilling, they can also become vehicles through which society restricts women's freedom and reduces them to the sum of these choices. The 4B movement challenges that reduction. By opting out of these expectations, women make a statement: if they can't make these choices freely, without strings attached, without judgment, without coercion, then maybe they shouldn't be making them.

At the heart of the 4B movement is the idea that genuine autonomy means more than just having the ability to make choices; it means making them for reasons that reflect one's values, dreams, and goals. For some, dating and marriage might feel like avenues for personal growth, mutual respect, and love. But for many others, these same paths come with unspoken pressures and societal controls. How many women have felt that marriage was less a choice than a "next step" they were expected to take? How many have felt pressured to have children because that's what women "do"? The 4B movement encourages women to consider these paths optional rather than obligatory. It asks us to question whether, under present conditions, these choices are indeed ours or if they've been subtly imposed by a society that has often cared more about women's roles than their well-being.

Another crucial part of the 4B philosophy is recognizing how these personal choices connect to more significant social dynamics. When we choose not to date, marry, or have children under compromised conditions, we're not just making decisions for ourselves; we're challenging a system that has long valued women based on their relationships with men and family roles. The decision to abstain is a form of peaceful protest, saying that we won't contribute to a society that doesn't value our independence. In that sense, 4B isn't anti-men or anti-family; it's anti-coercion. It's a movement that argues women should be able to make these choices without pressure, manipulation, or societal expectations, shaping what's supposed to be personal and sacred. For many, the 4B movement is about reclaiming their worth, not as someone's partner or mother but as their own person with dreams, goals, and autonomy that deserve respect.

Through the 4B movement, women stand for something beyond individual decisions. They're standing for a world where a woman's choices around love, sex, and motherhood are no longer treated as markers of her worth but as extensions of her freedom. Whether one's reasons for joining the movement are spiritual, political, or deeply personal, they all come back to one core belief: that a woman's life is her own, and she alone should decide what she wants to do with it. The 4B movement ultimately isn't just about saying "no" to certain things; it's about saying "yes" to a future where women's choices are free from judgment, manipulation, or control. It's about giving women back the power to define their lives on their own terms.

Eidotheosophy And The 4B Movement

When we look at the 4B movement through the lens of eidotheosophy, the concept of god's influence in biblical mythology takes on a nuanced depth. Eidotheosophy starts with the premise that some of biblical mythology's ideas and ethics may come from god's wisdom. Still, it also recognizes that humanity has woven its interests and biases into the fabric of religious texts. This framework asks us to separate divine wisdom from human interference, urging us to hold fast to god's truths while discarding what humanity has wrongly attributed to him. And when it comes to women's autonomy, this separation becomes critically important.

We encounter a spectrum of perspectives on women's roles and rights in biblical mythology. On the one hand, troubling passages frame women as property, as though their worth is tied to their utility to men. On the other hand, we see examples of women exercising full autonomy and authority, such as Deborah, a prophet and judge of Israel. These conflicting ideas raise a crucial question: which represents god's wisdom, and which is the result of humanity's attempt to control and dominate?

Eidotheosophy provides a guide here: god's wisdom aligns with justice, love, and the inherent dignity of all people. Ideas that degrade or diminish women's autonomy clearly reflect human interests, not divine will. History and science back this up. When we look at historical patterns and academic research, we see that societies that infringe on women's autonomy consistently experience deep injustices and inequities that ripple through every level of community and family life. These injustices aren't just spiritual failings; they're societal failures rooted in the misguided human desire to control rather than uplift.

The evidence is clear: restoring women's autonomy leads to profound societal benefits. Communities thrive when women can make their own choices about relationships, marriage, work, and reproduction. Research shows improvements in economic stability, better outcomes for children, and healthier, more equitable social structures. These findings don't contradict god's wisdom; they affirm it. They show that god's vision for humanity is mutual respect, freedom, and flourishing, not one where half of the population is subjugated to serve the other.

Through the lens of eidotheosophy, the 4B movement is not just a social or political stance; it's a spiritual one. It's a call to peel back the layers of human distortion and rediscover the divine truth that women's autonomy is a cornerstone of justice and equality. When we reject humanity's so-called "wisdom" and embrace god's vision, we create a world that reflects the love, fairness, and dignity he intended. And the evidence in biblical mythology and science tells us that this is the path toward a better, more just society for everyone.

Eidotheosophy And Resisting Injustice

When we approach the idea of resisting the status quo through the lens of eidotheosophy, we start with a foundational principle: god's influence is present in the mythology and teachings of biblical mythology, but the way humanity has interpreted and applied these teachings often reflects human wisdom rather than divine insight. Eidotheosophy suggests that some concepts and ideas may be genuinely inspired by god. Still, others are coloured by human biases, interpretations, and desires. This distinction is critical when we think about the justice of resistance and the role of movements like the 4B movement. If we acknowledge that divine wisdom is infused into certain biblical teachings and, at the same time, recognize that human interference often distorts god's intention, we are in a better position to challenge the status quo as a divine mandate for societal change.

God's call to confront injustice isn't merely about upholding established norms or following rules handed down by those in power. It's about pushing back against the systems that dehumanize people, particularly women, by refusing to conform to structures that strip away their autonomy. In the context of the 4B movement, this means challenging a societal framework that reduces women to their reproductive roles or pressures them into relationships that violate their agency. Historically, humanity has misinterpreted biblical mythology in ways that have served to oppress and control, particularly when it comes to women. But by returning to the essence of divine wisdom, without the layers of human distortion, we can see that god has always been on the side of justice and autonomy.

Eidotheosophy calls us to separate what god has revealed from what humanity has imposed, and in doing so, it invites us to reclaim a clearer understanding of god's will for human dignity. The mythology of biblical mythology presents stories of individuals like Moses and the prophets as examples who resisted oppressive powers because they were moved by god's desire for justice. Moses didn't confront Pharaoh out of personal vendetta or a willingness to challenge authority; he did so because he had a divine mandate to resist the institution of slavery to free the enslaved. Similarly, prophets like Amos called out societal injustices, urging people to "let justice roll down like waters." These acts of resistance weren't just acts of rebellion; they were expressions of divine justice rooted in the wisdom that calls for the flourishing of all people, especially the marginalized.

In light of this, the 4B movement can be considered part of that same divine resistance. The movement calls for women to refuse participation in societal roles where their autonomy is compromised, such as forced marriage, coerced sexual relationships, or being pressured into motherhood without choice. The 4B movement is more than a personal stand; it is an act of spiritual resistance to a system that has for too long denied women the freedom to govern their own lives. As part of a more significant societal shift, this refusal aligns with the biblical imperative to resist injustice, not through violence, but through nonviolent means, echoing the resistance modelled by figures like Moses or the prophets.

Incorporating eidotheosophy into this analysis helps us distinguish between what has been divinely inspired in biblical mythology and what has been corrupted by human interpretation. The 4B movement, through this lens, is not merely a challenge to a social norm; it is a direct challenge to the unjust systems that have been justified by distorted theological interpretations. The societal shift it aims for isn't just about equal rights; it's about aligning society with god's true purpose for justice and autonomy. In this framework, the 4B movement is not just a rebellion against an unjust status quo; it is a movement that reflects the very will of god, pushing society toward the respect and dignity that god has always intended for his creation, particularly women. Therefore, god supports the 4B movement because it mirrors the divine wisdom and justice woven into the fabric of biblical mythology, even if human history has sometimes obscured that truth.

God Endorses Autonomy And Dignity For Women

When we talk about the 4B movement and its foundation, I believe it's essential to understand that autonomy and dignity for women are values that align with god's teachings. To me, it's clear that god intends for all people to live with respect, freedom, and the right to make choices that honour their paths. God created every person with unique gifts and a purpose, and the idea of having dominion over our lives is not just a human instinct; it's a reflection of the divine image within us. I don't believe it's god's plan for women, or anyone, to live without agency or to be boxed into roles that diminish their worth. Instead, god calls us to stand in our full dignity, to make choices that come from the heart, and to avoid situations that compromise who we are at the core. This is precisely what the 4B movement seeks to uphold.

Throughout biblical mythology, there are countless examples where god encourages choice and honours the autonomy of individuals. Think of how often Jesus invited people to come to him of their own will or examples where god did not force obedience but instead presented choices and asked people to follow freely. This is why I see autonomy as a profoundly spiritual right. God respects free will, and with that, he emphasizes the worth and dignity of each person to make their own decisions. The 4B movement, which calls for women to abstain from relationships, marriage, and childbearing until their autonomy is respected, speaks directly to this respect for free will. It's not about rejecting love, commitment, or family; it's about choosing these things only when grounded in true freedom and respect. When society tries to control a woman's choices in these areas, it contradicts god's own way of dealing with humanity, with openness and a desire for choices made out of love, not obligation.

I believe god's stance on dignity and respect is woven into everything Jesus taught. He uplifted those who were marginalized, and he never treated women as if they were only valuable through marriage or motherhood. Jesus interacted with women as individuals; he saw their potential, their thoughts, and their questions. The women at the well, Mary and Martha, and Mary Magdalene, all were shown respect, regardless of whether they were wives, mothers, or neither. God doesn't see a woman's worth only in relation to these roles, and that's what the 4B movement reflects. This movement declares that a woman's value doesn't depend on her relationships with others, especially when those relationships can be shaped by societal expectations instead of her desires. Consider how Jesus himself could see and honour the dignity of women as individuals first. In that case, I feel confident that god supports women's autonomy, just as the 4B movement does.

In the 4B movement, we find a call for women to resist roles that don't feel freely chosen, and this aligns with god's desire for all of us to live authentic lives. There's a sacredness in saying "no" to expectations that limit us. Just as god values truth and wholeness, the 4B movement values women's right to be whole people, respected for their choices. When we honour autonomy, we honour the spirit of freedom god instilled in us. It's a way of saying that we are created as whole, complete beings who don't need marriage, a partner, or children to fulfill some societal checklist of what makes us valuable. It's not a rejection of these roles; it's a decision to pursue them only when they align with personal autonomy and dignity. By prioritizing this autonomy, women in the 4B movement are living out a belief that god supports: that love, relationships, and family are choices meant to be free, not forced.

And really, if god champions anything, it's the right to live as individuals who make choices out of love and freedom, not out of fear or pressure. Much of biblical mythology encourages us to live in a way that feels true to ourselves, in line with god's love. The 4B movement is one way women can reclaim this autonomy and resist any societal structures that don't respect it. Suppose a society or culture tries to reduce a woman's life to the roles she fills for others. In that case, it's not honouring her god-given dignity. Instead, the 4B movement pushes back on that, asserting that until a woman can enter into these roles freely and fully, without pressure or expectations to conform, she can, and perhaps should, choose to abstain. God designed us to live with freedom and respect, and the 4B movement aligns perfectly with that divine vision.

Opting Out Of Traditional Roles

The idea that women should opt out of traditional roles until society fully respects their autonomy isn't just a reaction to current issues; it's a stance grounded in spiritual, historical, and academic foundations that have long argued for justice and equality. I believe god's teachings value autonomy, dignity, and respect. We see this emphasis on choice and self-worth throughout biblical mythology, where people are encouraged to make decisions that honour their faith and individuality rather than conforming to imposed expectations. Jesus's interactions with women show this, too; he treated women as equal recipients of his message, not as mere extensions of men or limited to their societal roles. So, when society demands that women fit into traditional roles that deny them agency, opting out can be a robust, spiritually grounded response. It's a way of honouring each woman's god-given dignity.

Historically, we see countless examples of women who have resisted roles that limited them, often standing against societal norms to pursue lives that reflected their inner calling. The suffragists fought tirelessly for the right to vote because they knew their voices mattered. Or the women who pushed into higher education and professions where they were told they didn't belong, asserting their worth and skills in spaces where society had yet to make room for them. History shows us that progress only happens when people are willing to step back from traditions that confine them and demand better. The 4B movement continues this legacy, a modern-day example of women refusing roles that don't align with their self-worth. Just as these historical figures challenged the norms of their time, women in the 4B movement are choosing to wait until relationships, marriage, and family can be places of equality and mutual respect rather than avenues for social control.

From an academic standpoint, there's strong support for the idea that autonomy and respect are essential to well-being. Studies in psychology and sociology consistently show that when people are empowered to make life choices, their mental health, sense of fulfillment, and overall life satisfaction improve significantly. These findings aren't just numbers; they reflect a human need for autonomy and agency. Conversely, we know that when women are pressured into roles or relationships that don't honour their choices, it leads to frustration, stress, and even physical and emotional harm. Social scientists have long pointed out the damaging effects of these pressures, suggesting that traditional roles need re-evaluation in light of modern understandings of mental and social health. The 4B movement takes these findings seriously, advocating that women should choose traditional roles only when they're freely chosen, not forced by outdated structures.

This philosophy is deeply rooted in a call for justice and equality. It's not about rejecting relationships or family; it's about waiting until these institutions genuinely respect women's autonomy. Many laws and social expectations today still reflect outdated, patriarchal beliefs, where women's choices are limited by factors beyond their control. For instance, we still see how legal systems in some places fail to protect women's rights over their own bodies, their financial independence, or even their career choices. This lack of respect in legal and societal structures signals that the conditions for women to fully embrace traditional roles without compromise still need to be met. The 4B movement suggests that until those systems are reformed to uphold true equality, women should feel free to step back from roles that might otherwise strip them of their agency. This isn't a rejection of tradition for the sake of it; it's a call to reform tradition so that it aligns with justice, respect, and a modern understanding of human rights.

So, looking at the 4B movement through spiritual, historical, and academic lenses, it becomes clear that this philosophy has a solid moral foundation. It's not about dismissing relationships, family, or any other traditional role as inherently wrong. Instead, an ethical stance says that unless and until these roles respect a woman's autonomy, she is justified in opting out. Just as people throughout history have waited for the right conditions to make choices aligned with their values, women today abstain from traditional roles until they're offered the dignity and respect they deserve. It's a stance that has been long in the making, rooted in the belief that every person deserves the freedom to make their own choices.

Women's Intrinsic Value And Autonomy

When I think about biblical mythology, I see countless examples where god emphasizes the intrinsic value and autonomy of women, even when society around them failed to do so. From the start, the creation story speaks to this value; both men and women are made in the image of god, which means every woman's worth is sacred, inherent, and not tied to what she can do for others. She is valuable because she is a reflection of god. That powerful message sets the tone for how god sees women. He doesn't see them as mere helpers or subordinates; he sees them as fully realized beings, created with purpose and strength, just as they are. This idea of women's intrinsic value challenges the historical tendency to treat women as if they exist primarily to serve others, especially men. But in god's eyes, a woman's worth is woven into her very being.

Biblical mythology also shows us women who defy societal expectations to act with autonomy and courage. Take Deborah, for example; she was a judge and prophet who led Israel with wisdom and authority. Her story is a reminder that god calls women into leadership and respects their abilities to make critical, independent decisions. Deborah wasn't defined by her relationship with a man and didn't need someone else's permission to act. God valued her for her wisdom, strength, and faithfulness, and that's why she was entrusted with such a significant role. Then there's Ruth, whose loyalty and courage in deciding to stay with Naomi, her mother-in-law, was an act of love and commitment that came from her choice. Ruth's life choices went against what would have been expected or convenient. Yet, her story is celebrated as one of resilience and honour. These women weren't valued solely for traditional roles; they were valued for their choices, their faith, and their integrity.

One of the most profound moments highlighting women's worth comes from Jesus. He treated women as equals in a culture that often did not. In the story of the woman at the well, Jesus spoke to her openly and respected her intellect and spiritual curiosity, even though society marginalized her. He didn't judge her or reduce her worth to her past; instead, he offered her dignity and a direct invitation to faith, just as he did with any of his male disciples. In this simple conversation, Jesus affirmed her autonomy, giving her the respect to make her own choices about her faith.

Similarly, when Mary chose to sit at Jesus's feet and learn alongside his disciples, a place traditionally reserved for men, Jesus defended her choice. He told her sister Martha that Mary had chosen "the better part," emphasizing that women have every right to seek spiritual knowledge and fulfillment outside conventional roles. These stories clearly indicate that Jesus respected and uplifted women's autonomy and saw their value as individuals capable of making their own spiritual and life choices.

It's also worth mentioning Proverbs 31, a chapter often quoted for describing a "virtuous woman." But looking closer, the woman in this passage is much more than a quiet, subservient figure. She's industrious, making decisions for her household and managing finances and trade. She is praised for her wisdom, strength, and independence, all of which contribute to her value, not because she is fulfilling an external expectation but because she is embracing her gifts and using them in ways uniquely her own. God's vision for women is that they are capable, wise, and valued. Proverbs 31 underscores that a woman's worth comes from who she is and how she lives purposefully, not simply from fitting into a narrow role.

For me, these scriptural themes make it clear that god doesn't just tolerate women's autonomy; he encourages it. He sees women as whole individuals with the right to choose their paths, contribute to society, and express their faith in ways that reflect their true selves. Biblical mythology often highlights women's intrinsic value, courage, and wisdom, affirming their right to make choices that honour their dignity and calling. The god I believe in values women for who they are, not for what society thinks they should be.

Marriage As An Equal Partnership

When I look at the new testament's approach to marriage, I see a vision of partnership based on equality, respect, and mutual love, a view that stands in stark contrast to relationships where one partner is coerced or devalued. The new testament teaches that marriage isn't about rigid roles but about each person contributing fully and freely to the relationship. This is especially clear in the writings of Paul, who talks about marriage as a reflection of Christ's relationship with the Church in Ephesians. He calls both husbands and wives to mutual submission, emphasizing a spirit of love, humility, and selflessness. This doesn't describe a relationship where one partner holds power over the other. Instead, it paints a picture of two individuals respecting each other's humanity and bringing their best selves to the table.

Paul's idea of mutual submission is powerful because it suggests that both partners in a marriage are equally valuable and should act out of love, not obligation. When he tells husbands to love their wives "as Christ loved the church and gave himself up for her," he's talking about self-sacrificial love that honours and uplifts the other person rather than controls or limits them. This kind of love doesn't fit with any notion of coercion or dominance. Both partners should feel empowered, valued, and free to be themselves. Coercing a partner or diminishing their role contradicts this foundational concept of love that places value on both people. I don't believe god intended for marriage to become a tool for control or for one partner's will to override the other's autonomy. Instead, it's meant to be a relationship where both people support their growth and respect each other's choices.

Another key theme that reinforces marriage equality is how Jesus interacted with women. While Jesus never married, he modelled a relationship based on respect and mutual understanding in all his interactions. He never treated women as second-class or subordinate but engaged with them as equals. When Martha approached him to ask for help with her sister Mary, who chose to sit and learn rather than fulfill domestic duties, Jesus didn't scold Mary. Instead, he supported her choice, telling Martha that Mary's decision to learn was just as valuable as Martha's traditional role. This response from Jesus challenges the idea that specific roles are inherently "female" and must be followed. Instead, he honoured individual choices, suggesting that marriage, too, should celebrate both partners' freedom and equal worth. For me, this is a clear sign that any expectation for women to take on a lesser or undervalued role in marriage doesn't align with the values Jesus upheld.

In the new testament, we also find examples of women who actively participated in the early Church's life alongside men. Priscilla, for example, was a respected teacher and leader who worked with her husband, Aquila, as an equal in spreading the Gospel. Her role wasn't limited by her gender or marriage; instead, she and Aquila served together in a way that utilized their strengths and gifts. The fact that Priscilla was a recognized teacher in a religious context traditionally dominated by men speaks volumes about the value the early Church placed on her contributions. Her partnership with Aquila is a model of marriage where each person's talents and calling are honoured equally, showing that a marriage rooted in mutual respect and equality is not just a personal preference but a divine principle. If one partner's role is diminished or undervalued, that partnership loses the balance and mutual respect that god intended.

Even the new testament's concept of love reinforces this theme. The famous passage in 1 Corinthians 13 describes love as patient, kind, and not self-seeking. This description isn't just poetic; it's instructional, especially for relationships. Love that "does not insist on its own way" can't exist in a marriage where one partner's choices or individuality are constrained or undervalued. As Paul described, true love means allowing each person to be fully themselves, fostering an environment of support, freedom, and equal value. If a marriage dynamic strays from this kind of love and falls into patterns of control or coercion, it directly contradicts the biblical definition of love. God's principles for marriage don't endorse relationships where one partner is denied their full agency; instead, these principles call for a union where both people find strength in each other's autonomy.

This new testament vision of marriage as an equal partnership is a clear mandate against any form of coercion, undervaluing, or role enforcement that stifles one partner's autonomy. God didn't design marriage as a system of hierarchy or control. It is a partnership that reflects the love and mutual respect he shows to all of us. Any interpretation of marriage that encourages coercion or demands that one person submit to a devalued role misses the mark of god's design. Instead, I believe that god's vision is for marriage to be a place where both people are empowered, loved, and fully respected, where each partner is free to live out their calling and contribute equally to the relationship. This isn't just a modern ideal; it's a divine principle that goes back to the heart of the new testament's teachings on love and partnership.

Free Will As A Divine Gift

Free will is one of the most profound gifts god has given humanity. From the beginning, biblical mythology emphasizes our ability to make choices as an essential part of being human. God didn't create us as robots or mindless followers; instead, he gave us the ability to choose, knowing that our choices shape our character, define our relationships, and build our moral integrity. I believe this gift of free will is central to how we understand ourselves in our relationship with god. Suppose that god values our autonomy enough to give us the freedom to choose even between right and wrong. In that case, that freedom applies to every part of our lives, including the right for women to make choices about their own bodies, relationships, and futures.

In the story of Adam and Eve, we see free will in action. God places them in the Garden of Eden with clear instructions but also allows them the freedom to choose whether or not to follow those instructions. They aren't shielded from the possibility of making mistakes; instead, they're given the autonomy to decide, even though god knows it could lead to pain and struggle. To me, this demonstrates that choice itself has value to god. He respects our agency enough to let us exercise it fully. This isn't just about Adam and Eve; it's a fundamental principle that applies to each of us. It tells me that god values our right to choose and believes in our capacity to learn and grow from our decisions. And suppose god grants all humans this kind of autonomy. In that case, it includes women's right to control their lives without interference from societal pressures or external demands that try to override their choices.

Free will also plays a crucial role in our moral integrity. Without the freedom to choose, there's no real moral growth, no genuine virtue. Biblical mythology constantly highlights the importance of choice in building a life of faith and integrity. Each decision we make, whether about kindness, justice, or love, has moral weight because we are free to choose otherwise. We grow in faith because we actively choose god's ways, not because we're forced into them. In that sense, our choices reflect our values and beliefs, shaping us into the people we become. This principle equally applies to women's right to make life choices. When society tries to limit women's freedom, whether through cultural expectations, legal restrictions, or even subtle pressures, it undermines their ability to develop moral integrity on their own terms. Forcing a woman into a role or decision that isn't hers removes her chance to grow through her choices, robbing her of the dignity of making decisions for herself.

Jesus's teachings further emphasize the significance of free will and choice. He constantly invited people to follow him but never coerced them. He allowed them to choose, recognizing that authentic faith and love come only when they are freely given. Jesus invited people to make life-altering choices, but he respected their autonomy. For instance, the rich young ruler was given the option to sell his possessions and follow Jesus. Jesus didn't stop or force him to comply when he walked away. This shows us that Jesus valued free will as part of each person's spiritual journey. Women, too, deserve the same freedom to choose what is best for their lives without facing barriers undermining their autonomy.

I also see this respect for individual choice reflected in the concept of consent and the idea that love must be freely given. Consent isn't just a modern ethical principle; it's foundational to healthy relationships and aligns with god's view of love. God doesn't force us into a relationship with him. He invites us, respects our choices, and loves us unconditionally, whether or not we choose him. This model of divine love underscores the importance of respecting others' choices. Women's choices should be treated equally, especially in relationships, bodies, and futures. Any system that undermines this right to choose violates the very principles of consent, dignity, and freedom that we see modelled by god himself.

Theologically, free will is essential to the image of god within us. It's a divine trait that gives us the power to shape our lives and take responsibility for our choices. To deny women this autonomy, to suggest that they should be bound by predetermined roles or societal expectations, runs contrary to this core value. I believe that god's gift of choice is a reminder that every individual is worthy of respect and capable of deciding their path. This respect for free will is woven into much of biblical mythology, reminding us that autonomy is not just a right but a sacred part of being human. For women, this means that controlling their own lives and making their own choices about relationships, family, and their own bodies isn't just a social issue; it's a spiritual mandate that honours the god-given freedom and integrity within us.

A Historical Look At Women's Autonomy Undermined

When I think about the history of women's autonomy, it's honestly pretty disheartening to see how long societies have tried to limit women's freedom. In ancient times, women were often treated more like property than people. In many cultures, a woman's primary identity was tied to her father, husband, or male relatives. Her worth was often reduced to what she could bring as a dowry or how many children she could bear, particularly sons. For example, women's legal and social standing in ancient Greece was tightly controlled. A woman couldn't vote, own property in her name, or even choose her spouse in most cases. Marriage wasn't about mutual partnership or love but more about securing alliances and family honour. This isn't to say women didn't find ways to exercise their own power within these limitations, but the constraints on their autonomy were so heavy that their rights and self-determination were almost nonexistent. Society saw women as part of a man's assets rather than individuals with goals and desires.

This pattern of undermining women's autonomy continued throughout the Middle Ages and into early modern Europe, where women were often excluded from education and political life. Laws across various regions enforced women's legal dependence on men. Married women were subject to what was called "coverture" in England, which meant that legally, a woman's rights were "covered" by her husband; she essentially ceased to exist as a separate legal entity. A woman couldn't own property or sign contracts on her own. Her rights were effectively transferred to her husband. The idea that women couldn't be trusted to manage their own affairs was deeply embedded in law and custom, reinforcing the notion that they were somehow less capable than men. This wasn't just about money or property; it was about erasing women's personhood, making them invisible in the eyes of the law. The fact that marriage laws were designed to strip women of their autonomy tells me just how much society was invested in controlling every part of women's lives.

Even in times and places where women held a bit more power, like during the Renaissance when a few aristocratic women could become patrons of the arts or even rulers, the opportunities were rare and usually conditional. These exceptions are often held up as proof that women had autonomy. However, such was only the privilege of a very few and usually came with limitations or expectations that still placed women in a secondary role. For the average woman, life remained restricted. She was defined by her utility to her family, her obedience, and her ability to conform to societal norms.

In most cases, women were expected to marry, bear children, and maintain a household. Their influence was almost entirely confined within these boundaries. If a woman chose to step outside these expectations, she risked being labelled as deviant or sinful. History shows us time and again that society wasn't comfortable with women who had ambitions or goals beyond these roles, so they used laws, religion, and culture to suppress any hint of autonomy.

The struggle for autonomy persisted into the modern era, especially during the 19th and early 20th centuries, as more women began pushing for rights. The women's suffrage movement marked a significant shift, with women demanding political representation and the right to vote. For the first time, women publicly challenged the structures that had long confined them. Yet, even then, they faced fierce opposition. Many believed that women's place was still in the home and that granting them the right to vote or work outside the home would disrupt social order. This shows that society's grip on women's autonomy wasn't just a historical issue but something actively maintained. When women finally gained the right to vote, own property, and work in some professions, these rights were granted reluctantly and with countless restrictions. Society didn't fully embrace women's autonomy; it was a long, hard fight to gain a few fundamental freedoms that men had enjoyed without question.

In the present day, while women's rights have expanded significantly, the legacy of this long history of control still affects us. Women may be able to vote, work, and pursue careers. However, there are still cultural and structural barriers that limit their autonomy. Wage gaps, underrepresentation in leadership positions, and societal expectations about family and caregiving roles all reinforce the idea that women's autonomy is somehow secondary to men's. And when it comes to reproductive rights, we're still seeing society debate whether women should have the freedom to make decisions about their own bodies. It's a direct link to those earlier times when women were considered property, with their bodies and choices controlled by others. The fact that we're still arguing over these fundamental freedoms tells me that, as far as we've come, we're still wrestling with the same outdated beliefs about women's autonomy.

From ancient laws that treated women as property to modern systems that still restrict our choices, this history has a clear message: society has been deeply invested in keeping women from having complete control over their own lives. This isn't just a relic of the past but a pattern we can see continuing in different forms today. Looking at how long and fiercely society has worked to limit women's autonomy, it becomes clear why movements like the 4B movement are necessary. The push for women to reject marriage, dating, and childbearing until their autonomy is respected isn't just a reaction to modern problems; it's a stand against a long history of oppression. It's a call to reclaim the rights that should never have been denied in the first place, to finally break free from a pattern that has held women back for centuries.

The Influence Of Patriarchy On Law And Religion

When I think about the ways patriarchy has used religion to control women, it becomes clear just how deeply embedded these ideas are in both our laws and cultural norms. Religion has always been a powerful force in shaping societies, giving people a sense of meaning and community. But historically, those in power have often twisted religious doctrine to justify controlling others, especially women. Men who held religious and political authority frequently interpreted doctrine to reinforce their power, setting up a social order where women were expected to be submissive, obedient, and limited in their roles. The result has been centuries of systemic control, where patriarchy has not just been a social structure but has been woven into the moral fabric of societies, with religion providing the rationale for keeping women in subordinate positions.

The use of religious doctrine to enforce these ideas started early, with interpretations of texts that placed men in authority over women. Take the story of Adam and Eve, for instance. Many religious leaders have long used this story to suggest that women are inherently flawed or that their role is to be subservient to men. They often point to Eve's temptation as proof that women are more susceptible to sin, using this as a reason to keep women out of positions of influence or authority. This interpretation suggests that women must be "protected" or "controlled" to prevent moral failure. In reality, this reading of the story has less to do with divine truth and more to do with keeping power in the hands of men. It's a selective interpretation that ignores biblical mythology's broader themes of free will and redemption, focusing instead on a single narrative used to justify control.

As societies became more structured, laws directly reflected these patriarchal interpretations of religious doctrine. In many cultures, religious institutions influenced laws that restricted women's autonomy, embedding the idea of male authority into legal systems. For instance, marriage laws in various cultures have historically required women to obey their husbands. At the same time, men were granted legal control over their wives' property, finances, and even bodies. These laws didn't just reflect the culture of the time; they were often justified through religious teachings that promoted male dominance. Over centuries, religious leaders and lawmakers worked together, framing these restrictions as god's design for society. Women's roles were defined as supportive, domestic, and secondary to men's, implying that this structure was divinely sanctioned. This approach effectively erased women's individual rights and autonomy, making it difficult for them to assert control over their own lives without facing both legal and social condemnation.

One of the most striking examples of religion being used to control women is the concept of modesty. Across various religions, teachings on modesty have been applied much more strictly to women than to men, often with the claim that women's bodies are a source of temptation and, therefore, need to be covered or hidden. In many societies, this has led to strict dress codes for women, reinforcing the idea that women are responsible for controlling men's desires. The underlying message is that women's bodies are inherently problematic, something to be regulated rather than celebrated. This perspective doesn't come from any inherent moral or spiritual truth; it's a way for patriarchal structures to exert control, to keep women focused on conforming to a particular standard rather than exploring their own identities or autonomy. By placing the burden of modesty on women, these doctrines enforce a subtle form of control that affects how women see themselves and limits their freedom to express their individuality.

Religious doctrine has also been used to enforce the idea that a woman's primary purpose is to marry and bear children. This concept, present in religious teachings and societal expectations, has historically been framed as a divine calling. While the role of mother and wife might be a fulfilling path for many women, when this role is presented as the only "godly" option, it limits women's choices and stifles their potential. Many religious institutions have promoted the idea that women who pursue careers, remain single, or choose not to have children are somehow rejecting their divine purpose. This perspective must recognize that each person's calling is unique and that women, like men, have individual talents, desires, and goals that may or may not include traditional family roles. By defining women's purpose narrowly, religious doctrine has often been used to guilt or pressure women into lives that may not align with their true selves, reinforcing a system where women are valued primarily for their roles as wives and mothers rather than as individuals with their own gifts and callings.

Even within the church, patriarchy has shaped the roles that women are allowed to take on. Many religious organizations still restrict women from positions of leadership or spiritual authority, citing scripture as justification. The irony here is that the same religious texts that are used to limit women also contain examples of women who led, taught, and held positions of influence. Figures like Deborah in the old testament, a prophet and judge, or Priscilla in the new testament, an influential teacher in the early church, demonstrate that women's leadership has always had a place in spiritual communities. However, patriarchal interpretations have consistently downplayed these examples, focusing instead on selective passages that reinforce male authority. This selective reading isn't about honouring divine truth; it's about maintaining power dynamics that favour men. By limiting women's roles within religious spaces, these doctrines not only restrict women's spiritual growth but also send a message that women's insights, wisdom, and contributions are somehow less valuable.

Recently, some religious institutions have adapted as women have pushed for more autonomy. Still, the remnants of these patriarchal interpretations remain deeply rooted. Even today, religious arguments are often used to oppose women's rights to make decisions about their bodies, careers, and personal lives. Issues like reproductive rights are frequently framed as moral or religious concerns, with arguments that ignore women's autonomy and reduce complex personal decisions to a matter of doctrine. These arguments continue to wield religious influence as a means of control, suggesting that a woman's personal choices must align with traditional beliefs rather than her own convictions. The reality is that these doctrines were never meant to be about moral guidance; they are tools used to maintain a social order where men remain in control, and women's autonomy is limited.

Looking at this long history, it's clear that patriarchy has consistently used religion as a way to justify restricting women's freedom. By framing control as a "divine mandate," these structures have forced women into roles and behaviours that often conflict with their own desires, gifts, and autonomy. It's a powerful reminder that true faith isn't about conforming to someone else's interpretation but about seeking a relationship with god that honours each person's unique purpose and potential. Faith should inspire freedom, dignity, and respect for all individuals, not be a tool to enforce inequality.

The Fight For Women's Rights

When I think about movements throughout history that have fought for women's rights, I'm reminded of how long and hard women have had to fight just for the most basic freedoms and recognition of their autonomy. The suffrage movement, which took place in the late 19th and early 20th centuries, is one of the earliest and most significant examples of this struggle. Women demanded the right to vote, but more than that, they demanded recognition as equal citizens capable of making decisions for themselves. They were challenging the very structure of society that had long held that women were too "delicate" or "unsuited" for political power. Women like Susan B. Anthony, Elizabeth Cady Stanton, and Alice Paul worked tirelessly, often facing ridicule and even imprisonment, all for the right to have a say in the laws that governed their lives. The suffrage movement was about much more than just voting; it was about recognizing women as individuals with their own voices and choices worthy of being heard in the public sphere. The 4B movement builds on this same foundation, insisting that women's autonomy should be respected in terms of voting rights and across every area of their lives, particularly in relationships and reproductive choices.

Then, you get to second-wave feminism, which took off in the 1960s and 1970s. This movement was about more than just giving women the right to vote. It focused on gender equality in every sense, workplace rights, reproductive rights, sexual liberation, and the fight against domestic violence and sexual harassment. It challenged traditional notions of femininity and pushed for women to have the ability to define their own roles. Leaders like Betty Friedan, Gloria Steinem, and Audre Lorde pushed against the idea that women's only place was in the home, advocating for women to have a voice in everything from politics to work to sexual relationships. Second-wave feminists recognized that women's liberation was intrinsically linked to their ability to make choices about their own bodies and lives. The 4B movement carries this fight forward, insisting that until women's bodies and reproductive abilities are seen as something they can control and use according to their own desires, they should have the right to step out of the roles that society tries to push them into. It's not just about women being allowed to choose; it's about society recognizing that women's choices are theirs and not to be dictated by anyone, whether family, religion, or law.

In modern times, we're seeing more intersectional autonomy movements, recognizing the varied experiences and struggles women face based on race, class, sexuality, and other factors. These movements are focused on challenging the structures that limit women's choices and opportunities. We've seen women from all over the world rise up in the #MeToo movement, for example, to expose the sexual harassment and violence that women face in every sphere of life. It's about confronting a deeply entrenched culture of silence and complicity and pushing for a future where women are free to control their bodies and lives without fear of exploitation or abuse. The 4B movement fits into this more significant cultural push for freedom and autonomy. Women demand a say in how they live their lives, who they choose to be with, and what they decide to do with their bodies. Just as modern autonomy movements challenge societal norms and legal structures, the 4B movement calls for women to opt out of systems that fail to honour their autonomy, especially regarding relationships, marriage, and childbearing.

Another connection can be drawn to the reproductive rights movement. Women's right to choose has been an ongoing battle, especially in the United States, where debates over abortion and birth control are still very much alive. The fight for reproductive rights isn't just about the right to terminate a pregnancy; it's about the larger question of who gets to decide what women do with their bodies. For centuries, women were seen as vessels for reproduction, their bodies not their own but tools for societal and familial needs. The 4B movement acknowledges that women's bodies should not be treated as vessels for anyone else's purposes but that women are autonomous, sovereign entities. The movement insists that women have the right to make all decisions about their reproductive health, free from state or societal interference. This idea of reclaiming autonomy over one's body is at the heart of the 4B movement, just as it has been central to reproductive rights struggles throughout history.

In some ways, the 4B movement is a natural evolution of these earlier efforts. It doesn't just seek equality in the traditional sense; it aims to upend the structures that have restricted women's freedom for centuries. It's not just about pushing for women's right to marry who they want or to work in any job they choose, though those are certainly important goals. It's about recognizing that these choices cannot be meaningful unless women are free to choose whether to engage in relationships, marriage, or childbearing. The 4B movement connects to the broader struggle for women's autonomy, building on the foundation of the suffrage movement, second-wave feminism, and modern autonomy movements that challenge traditional roles and patriarchal control. It's a recognition that true freedom for women isn't just about legal rights or economic opportunity but about the ability to make decisions about one's body and life without being constrained by outdated norms, laws, or societal expectations. This is the world that the 4B movement aims to create, where women are free to decide what they want their lives to look like, no longer beholden to roles and relationships that diminish their autonomy or worth.

Psychological And Sociological Impacts Of Denying Autonomy

When I think about the psychological and sociological impacts of denying women autonomy, it's clear that the effects are profound, long-lasting, and often damaging. Studies on mental health have consistently shown that when women are deprived of control over their relationships, bodies, and reproduction, they experience higher levels of stress, depression, and anxiety. Women who are expected to conform to traditional gender roles, whether in marriage, motherhood, or the workplace, often report feeling trapped, unfulfilled, and disempowered. This stress isn't just about personal dissatisfaction; it also affects physical health. Chronic stress, frequently linked to the lack of agency, can lead to a range of issues, from cardiovascular problems to weakened immune systems. When women are pressured into roles that don't align with their desires or values, the mental and physical toll is undeniable. The emotional labour involved in constantly performing a role that doesn't feel true to oneself is exhausting and corrosive, leading to a loss of self-esteem and, in many cases, a diminished sense of purpose. The 4B movement advocates for women's right to refuse relationships and reproductive roles that compromise their autonomy. It is about breaking this cycle and allowing women to thrive in ways that align with their authentic selves.

It's not just the psychological impact that is important here; there are also significant social and economic benefits when women can decide for themselves. Research has consistently shown that the entire society benefits when women have control over their personal decisions, whether choosing a career, delaying or forgoing marriage, or deciding when and if to have children. For instance, countries that prioritize gender equality in education and the workforce tend to see higher levels of economic growth, innovation, and social stability. When women can contribute fully to the economy, they bring unique perspectives and talents that drive progress. This is not only true on a macroeconomic level; the social benefits are equally clear. When women have access to education, healthcare, and employment opportunities, they are more likely to invest in their families and communities. They're better equipped to make decisions that improve their lives and children, leading to improved health outcomes, lower poverty rates, and greater social cohesion. In societies where women are empowered to make choices about their bodies and futures, far-reaching positive effects ripple outwards, creating more robust, prosperous communities.

The transformative power of women's autonomy can be seen in many regions worldwide where women have been given more control over their lives. One of the clearest examples is the rise of women's participation in the workforce and politics in Scandinavian countries. Countries like Sweden, Norway, and Finland have not only embraced policies that promote gender equality but have also shown the tangible benefits of women's autonomy. These nations have high rates of female participation in the workforce, with women holding leadership positions in business and government, and they consistently rank high in terms of quality of life, education, and healthcare. These countries' economic and social prosperity can be directly linked to the high level of women's independence and the supportive policies that allow women to make personal decisions that suit their lives and aspirations. These countries understand that when women are empowered to control their bodies, reproduction, and career paths, society benefits. The 4B movement resonates with this thinking; it advocates for women's right to choose self-governance, creating a more dynamic, prosperous, and equal society.

Looking further afield, we can also point to countries in the Global South where women's autonomy has led to significant social change. For instance, in Rwanda, after the 1994 genocide, women took on critical roles in rebuilding the country. Today, Rwanda has one of the highest percentages of women in parliament worldwide. This shift wasn't just about political representation; it was about women taking control of their futures and contributing to rebuilding their society. This shift's social and economic impact has been profound, with Rwanda's economy rapidly growing, poverty rates decreasing, and gender equality becoming a model for the region. Women in Rwanda are making decisions for themselves, their communities, and the nation as a whole. The economic and social prosperity that has followed the expansion of women's roles in Rwanda is a clear example of what happens when women are allowed to decide for themselves.

Similarly, in countries like Bangladesh, where microfinance institutions like Grameen Bank have empowered women to start their own businesses and contribute to the economy, we've seen significant shifts in poverty reduction and economic development. Microloans, which are often targeted specifically at women, allow them to create and run businesses, gain financial independence, and make decisions that improve not just their own lives but the lives of their families. The success of these programs shows the powerful economic benefits of supporting women's autonomy. When women are given the tools to control their financial destinies, they are not only able to lift themselves out of poverty, but they also become drivers of broader economic growth and social change.

These case studies underscore the same point: when women have control over their lives, they are not just benefiting themselves but contributing to the greater good. Whether through greater economic productivity, more stable societies, or more innovative solutions to complex problems, women's autonomy is a critical factor in societal transformation. The 4B movement, with its call for women to opt out of traditional roles undermining their autonomy, is not just a philosophical stance but a practical one. By allowing women to control their bodies, relationships, and reproduction, we set the stage for a more prosperous, equitable, and just society. These case studies, both historical and contemporary, show that when women are free to make their own choices, society as a whole thrives. This is the wisdom behind the 4B movement: it's not just a demand for women's rights; it's a call for societal progress through women's empowerment.

Marriage And Reproduction As Spiritual Choices

When we think about marriage and reproduction, it's easy to fall into the trap of viewing them as mandatory societal norms that every woman is expected to follow. But, when examining biblical mythology, we see that marriage and reproduction are spiritual choices, not mandates. Biblical mythology presents both marriage and childbearing as blessings but not as obligations, especially when they involve sacrificing one's autonomy. There is a profound spiritual truth in recognizing that these choices should be made from personal conviction and discernment rather than societal or religious pressure. The 4B movement, at its core, advocates for the idea that women should not feel coerced into marriage or reproduction, especially when these choices compromise their autonomy. Instead, we can look at biblical mythology to understand that while these aspects of life can be seen as blessings, they seem like they were never meant to be imposed as commandments, particularly when autonomy is compromised.

When biblical mythology discusses childbearing, it often refers to it as a blessing. Psalm 127:3 says, "Children are a heritage from the Lord, offspring a reward from him." In this light, childbearing is seen as a blessing and a gift from god. However, it's crucial to note that this blessing is not intended to be a commandment or a societal obligation. The context of this blessing is essential; it assumes that the decision to bear children is freely chosen, not forced upon someone due to societal or legal pressures. When women are denied control over their reproductive choices, this can create an environment where the blessing of children turns into a burden. Suppose we view reproduction as a spiritual choice. In that case, god's vision for it is one of freedom, not one where women are coerced into fulfilling a role that doesn't reflect their personal desires or autonomy. The 4B movement fits within this vision because it encourages women to opt out of childbearing if they feel their autonomy would be compromised in the process.

Paul's teachings in the new testament provide further insight into this discussion, especially when we consider his thoughts on singleness and celibacy. In 1 Corinthians 7:7, Paul writes, "I wish that all of you were as I am. But each of you has your own gift from god; one has this gift, another has that." Paul emphasizes that singleness and celibacy are valid life choices, and he even goes so far as to say that they can be advantageous for those who can live without the distractions of marriage and family. For Paul, the decision to remain single is not seen as a failure or a lack of fulfillment but as a legitimate and valuable way to live. This is incredibly important when we think about the pressures that women face in society to marry and bear children. Paul affirms that individuals should make decisions based on their gifts, desires, and discernment. There is no scriptural mandate that requires women to marry or have children; these decisions are to be made based on personal choice and spiritual conviction. The 4B movement aligns with Paul's teachings because it asserts that women have the right to choose their own paths in life, whether that means remaining single, choosing celibacy, or opting out of reproduction if these decisions align with their values and desires.

Regarding childbearing, it's also essential to consider the context of mutual respect and consent in biblical mythology. In a marriage, biblical mythology emphasizes mutual respect and love, such as in Ephesians 5:21, "Submit to one another out of reverence for Christ." This mutual submission isn't about one partner having power over the other but a shared respect and partnership. The decision to have children, therefore, should not be a one-sided choice or something forced upon a woman. Like any other significant life decision, childbearing should be a process of mutual respect, love, and consent between partners. If a woman is coerced into bearing children against her will, or if societal structures place the burden of reproduction solely on women, this is a violation of the principles of mutual respect and consent that are foundational to a spiritual understanding of relationships. The 4B movement supports the idea that women should be free to opt out of childbearing if it feels like an act of coercion or an imposition on their autonomy. This decision is not just personal; it's a spiritual stance against being forced into a role that undermines one's agency and dignity.

By framing childbearing as a blessing but not a commandment, we can see how the spiritual choice to opt out of marriage or reproduction aligns with the principles of biblical mythology. It's not about rejecting the blessings of family or relationships; it's about recognizing that these choices should be made freely, without the weight of coercion or the denial of autonomy. For women who feel that their autonomy would be compromised in these areas, opting out becomes not just a personal decision but a spiritual one. It's a stance that aligns with god's vision of individual freedom and dignity, where women are encouraged to make decisions based on their own gifts, desires, and relationship with god, not based on societal expectations or legal mandates. The 4B movement, at its core, echoes this spiritual truth: women should have the autonomy to choose their own paths, whether embracing marriage and childbearing as blessings or opting out entirely to preserve their autonomy and integrity.

When we look at biblical mythology, we see numerous examples of individuals who used nonviolent resistance to challenge oppressive systems and stand firm in their beliefs. These figures didn't resort to violence or force to assert their autonomy; instead, they relied on courage, wisdom, and faith to confront systems that sought to diminish their dignity and freedom. This is something that resonates deeply with the core values of the 4B movement, which advocates for women to opt out of systems and structures that undermine their autonomy, such as marriage, childbearing, or reproductive control, when these choices are coerced or imposed. Just as biblical figures resisted oppression through nonviolence, the 4B movement calls for resistance that preserves the dignity and integrity of all women, empowering them to make choices about their lives that align with their values and beliefs.

An important example of nonviolent resistance comes from the story of Esther. Esther, a Jewish woman who became queen of Persia, found herself in a position to challenge the systemic oppression faced by her people. When the king's advisor, Haman, devised a plan to annihilate the Jewish people, Esther didn't pick up a sword or rally an army. Instead, she used her position, intelligence, and courage to confront the king with the truth of Haman's plot. Esther risked her life to speak out, but she did so with a deep understanding that nonviolent resistance could be as powerful as violent rebellion. Through her actions, Esther demonstrated that standing up to oppressive systems doesn't always require brute force; it can be a strategic, peaceful form of resistance that upholds the dignity of all people. Similarly, the 4B movement encourages women to resist societal pressures to conform to traditional roles, such as marriage or motherhood, when these roles compromise their autonomy. This resistance doesn't have to be loud or violent; it can be an act of quiet, dignified refusal to comply with systems that don't honour one's right to choose.

The story of Jesus is, of course, the ultimate example of nonviolent resistance. Throughout his life, Jesus rejected the systems of power that sought to control and oppress people. He confronted the religious and political authorities of his time. Still, he did so with nonviolent methods, through teaching, parables, and healing, showing compassion to those who were marginalized. His ultimate act of resistance came on the cross, where he chose to bear the weight of oppression and injustice rather than resort to violence. Jesus didn't take up arms to overthrow the Roman Empire or the religious elite; instead, he offered a radical, nonviolent vision of god's kingdom, where love, peace, and respect for others were the guiding principles. The 4B movement aligns with this radical stance of resistance, encouraging women to reject systems that deny their autonomy but to do so in a way that maintains their dignity and nonviolent principles. Just as Jesus demonstrated through his life that true power comes from love, respect, and faith, the 4B movement shows that women's true path to liberation respects their right to choose without resorting to violent or harmful means.

Finally, the story of Daniel and his friends, Shadrach, Meshach, and Abednego, offers another powerful example of nonviolent resistance. These men refused to bow down to the king's statue, an act that would have violated their faith. They chose to face punishment rather than comply with an oppressive law that went against their beliefs. What's striking about their resistance is that it wasn't violent; they didn't take up arms against the king or the system. Instead, they stood firm in their faith and refused to compromise their integrity. In the context of the 4B movement, women are encouraged to take a similar stance when faced with oppressive expectations surrounding marriage and reproduction. Like Daniel and his friends, women can stand firm in their values and autonomy, rejecting societal pressure without resorting to violence or hostility. Their refusal to comply, even at significant personal cost, is a powerful reminder that resistance doesn't always have to be forceful; it can be a simple, peaceful refusal to accept an unjust status quo.

These examples of nonviolent resistance show that we don't need violence to confront oppressive systems. Instead, we can use our voices, actions, and faith to challenge those systems and assert our autonomy. Just as Esther, Jesus, and Daniel stood firm in the face of oppression, women can resist systems that deny their autonomy in a way that honours their dignity and upholds peaceful, nonviolent principles. The 4B movement is rooted in this resistance, which demands respect for women's autonomy and personal choices without violence or confrontation. It's a resistance that is not only spiritually sound but also aligned with biblical teachings of justice, freedom, and the dignity of all individuals.

Refusing To Participate As A Moral Stand

Refusing participation in traditional societal roles, especially those that infringe on a woman's autonomy, is a decisive moral stand that aligns deeply with nonviolent resistance. By encouraging women to abstain from dating, marriage, reproduction, or sex under circumstances where their autonomy is compromised, the 4B movement takes a deliberate stance against a system that seeks to control women's lives. This isn't about rejecting relationships or family structures outright but about recognizing when those systems have become tools of oppression. The abstentions within the 4B movement are not acts of passivity or withdrawal; instead, they serve as a direct moral protest against a society that expects women to conform to outdated and restrictive roles. Much like nonviolent resistance throughout history, the 4B movement's stance is an active form of refusal, refusing to accept a world that doesn't honour women's full dignity, autonomy, and personhood.

When we think about nonviolent resistance, we often think of iconic moments in history where individuals have chosen to stand firm against unjust systems through civil disobedience. The 4B movement takes a page from this tradition by advocating for nonparticipation in systems that perpetuate control over women's bodies and reproductive rights. This isn't about creating chaos or inciting violence; it's about asserting that women should have the right to make their own decisions about their bodies and lives, free from societal pressure. Just like the civil rights movement used nonviolent protest to challenge racial segregation, the 4B movement uses abstention as a method of moral protest, refusing to participate in systems that force women into roles that strip away their personal agency. The refusal to date, marry, have children, or engage in sex when one's autonomy is at risk is not a retreat from society; it is a stand for freedom and self-determination, which are foundational to both moral integrity and spiritual wholeness.

This kind of moral protest draws clear parallels to the actions of those who have historically fought against oppressive systems without resorting to violence. Consider the example of Mahatma Gandhi's nonviolent resistance to British colonial rule in India. Gandhi didn't call for armed conflict; he called for peaceful noncompliance with the oppressive laws that sought to control the lives of the Indian people. Similarly, the 4B movement doesn't call for rebellion or chaos but for women to refuse participation in a system that seeks to control and limit their choices. It calls for spiritual and moral integrity, encouraging women to take control of their own narratives rather than allowing their stories to be dictated by a society that often does not have their best interests at heart. By choosing abstention, women are not being passive; they are actively resisting the societal pressure to conform to roles that do not honour their personal autonomy.

In many ways, the 4B movement is akin to the boycotts and acts of civil disobedience that have defined some of the most significant movements in history. In the same way that Rosa Parks' refusal to give up her seat on the bus became a powerful act of defiance against systemic racial inequality, the choice for women to abstain from traditional roles becomes a moral protest against societal structures that do not allow for true freedom and autonomy. It's a refusal to accept the status quo, and it challenges the very idea that women's bodies, choices, and futures should be controlled by anyone other than the women themselves. Just as nonviolent resistance was essential in the civil rights movement, the 4B movement's abstention became crucial in the fight for women's liberation and empowerment.

At the heart of this resistance is the belief that women should be allowed to make choices that align with their values rather than being pushed into roles because of societal expectations or outdated traditions. The 4B movement's refusal to participate in traditional systems of marriage and reproduction is an act of moral clarity; it's a refusal to accept systems that perpetuate gender inequality, and instead, it's a commitment to the belief that women's lives should be governed by their own choices. This resistance can be seen as a moral protest, not just against the structures themselves but against the idea that women's autonomy can or should be negotiable.

Just as nonviolent resistance has changed the course of history in numerous contexts, the 4B movement offers a way for women to assert their moral right to choose, refuse participation in a system that doesn't honour their autonomy, and take a stand against the control of their bodies. The abstention isn't just about rejecting something; it's about affirming the right to choose freely, without coercion or pressure. In this way, the 4B movement is a spiritual and moral stand that seeks to protect women's autonomy and challenges the societal forces that continue to marginalize and control women's choices. It's a call to women everywhere to embrace their god-given right to decide their own paths, free from the constraints of a society that too often places their value in the roles they play for others rather than in the inherent dignity of their personhood.

The Power Of Collective Refusal

The power of collective refusal is a principle that has been proven time and time again in history, from Gandhi's Salt March to the Civil Rights Movement's boycotts. What makes these non-cooperation movements so powerful is their ability to disrupt systems of oppression through the simple yet profound act of refusing to participate. When individuals, or entire groups, collectively withdraw their support or participation in unjust systems, they create an undeniable ripple effect that often forces society to take notice and reconsider the status quo. The same principle applies to the 4B movement. The movement taps into a long-standing tradition of social impact through non-cooperation by advocating for women to collectively refuse participation in societal structures that undermine their autonomy, such as traditional roles of marriage and motherhood. Just as Gandhi's Salt March challenged the British Empire's control over salt production, the 4B movement challenges the societal structures that seek to control women's bodies and futures, calling on women to withhold their participation until their autonomy was respected.

Take, for example, the Civil Rights Movement in the United States. The boycotts, particularly the Montgomery Bus Boycott, demonstrated the power of collective refusal to change an oppressive system. When Black Americans collectively chose not to use public transportation in Montgomery, they sent a powerful message to the rest of the nation: the system was unjust, and it would not stand. It wasn't a violent protest or an attempt to forcefully tear down the system. Instead, it was an act of moral clarity, a refusal to continue participating in a system that perpetuated inequality and oppression. The same approach can be applied to the 4B movement, where women collectively choose to withhold their participation in a societal system that demands their roles be limited to marriage, motherhood, and subservience. By opting out, women in the movement don't just stop conforming to oppressive norms; they actively challenge those norms, demonstrating that they won't settle for a system that does not honour their full autonomy.

What's crucial about these movements is that their power lies in numbers. When a critical mass of people collectively refuse to comply, the force of their non-cooperation becomes almost impossible to ignore. This collective refusal challenges the foundation of oppressive systems, forcing society to adapt or face widespread disruption. In the case of women's collective refusal, this could mean a shift in how society views women's roles, where the expectation of marriage, motherhood, and subordination is replaced by a recognition of women as fully autonomous individuals with the right to make their own choices. Studies on collective action show that such movements are highly effective, particularly when they disrupt an institution's ability to function. By opting out, women in the 4B movement aren't just making individual decisions; they're making a statement that has the potential to challenge societal structures on a much broader scale.

Another example of the power of collective refusal can be found in the suffrage movements worldwide. Women's refusal to accept second-class citizenship and their collective action in demanding the right to vote led to widespread social and political change. In many cases, suffragists faced immense pushback. Still, their refusal to comply with the norms that sought to exclude them from the political process profoundly impacted them. The movement was rooted in the idea that women's autonomy was not negotiable and that they had the right to determine their place in society, just as men did. The 4B movement draws on that same foundational belief. Still, it takes the idea of autonomy further, questioning women's participation in societal systems. By collectively refusing to participate in systems that perpetuate gender inequality, women challenge not only the expectation of traditional roles but also the very framework that supports these roles.

The academic research on non-cooperation movements highlights several key factors that make these actions so effective. First, collective refusal forces the dominant system to acknowledge the power and will of those opting out. It forces institutions to deal with the reality that their control systems are being undermined. Second, non-cooperation often leads to a shift in public opinion. As more and more people join the movement, the cause becomes less about individual rebellion and more about a widespread moral movement. This is particularly relevant for the 4B movement, as women who refuse to comply with traditional societal roles can help shift the narrative, making it clear that the denial of women's autonomy is not acceptable. Over time, these acts of collective refusal can lead to fundamental changes in how society views women's roles, ultimately creating a cultural shift toward greater equality and respect for women's autonomy.

Non-cooperation movements also have a unique ability to engage with the moral consciousness of society. When people collectively refuse to participate in an unjust system, it forces society to ask questions about the morality of that system. This is where the 4B movement's abstentions are particularly powerful. By refusing to participate in societal expectations around marriage, sex, and reproduction, women in the movement are making a moral stand. This stand says, "We will not participate in systems that diminish our value and autonomy." This creates an opportunity for broader societal reflection. When enough people engage in collective refusal, it becomes impossible for society to ignore the moral implications of its actions. Just as boycotts and nonviolent protests have historically led to social and legal changes, the collective refusal of women to participate in systems that don't honour their autonomy can bring about transformative shifts in how women's rights are viewed and respected.

In many ways, the power of collective refusal is about reclaiming agency. It's about making a collective choice to stop participating in systems that force women into roles they do not choose. Academic research and historical examples demonstrate that when enough people opt out, a wave of social change cannot be easily dismissed. The 4B movement, through its call for women to collectively abstain from traditional societal roles, taps into this powerful principle of non-cooperation, showing how women's collective autonomy can be a catalyst for widespread societal transformation. Through the power of collective refusal, women can reshape the very structures that seek to control them, shifting the balance toward a society that recognizes and honours their inherent dignity and autonomy.

Considering Spiritual Womanhood For Today's World

When discussing "spiritual womanhood," it's crucial to separate the myths built around this concept from the deeper, more empowering truths in biblical mythology. Far too often, biblical womanhood has been framed in a restrictive, one-dimensional way that emphasizes submission, passivity, and service to others at the expense of a woman's autonomy. This version of biblical womanhood is used to enforce rigid roles for women. These roles often leave little room for self-respect, personal agency, or meaningful choice. But when you dig into biblical mythology, you find many examples that support a woman's right to respect herself, make her own decisions, and shape her life in partnership with god. In the new testament, we also see the example of women like Priscilla, a teacher and leader in the early church. In Acts 18, we read about how she worked alongside her husband, Aquila, to teach Apollos more accurately about the gospel. She wasn't confined to a supportive role behind the scenes; she was a teacher and a leader, taking the initiative to use her gifts and intellect to spread the message of Christ. This is a far cry from the narrow, traditional view of womanhood that suggests women should be quiet, subservient, and relegated to domestic tasks. Priscilla's example shows that being a spiritual woman doesn't mean relinquishing leadership or the ability to teach but instead using your unique gifts and abilities to contribute to the world around you.

Another misconception about spiritual womanhood is that a woman's value is tied to her relationship with a man or her role as a wife and mother. While biblical mythology indeed affirms the importance of marriage and family, it never suggests that a woman's identity should be defined solely by her relationship with men. Proverbs 31, often cited as the ultimate guide to "biblical womanhood," actually emphasizes a woman's wisdom, strength, and dignity in her own right. Proverbs 31:25

says, "She is clothed with strength and dignity; she can laugh at the days to come." This isn't a woman defined by others but a woman who defines herself. Her worth isn't in her ability to serve others but in her character, wisdom, and strength. This passage affirms that women should be free to define their own lives, whether being a wife and mother or living independently and pursuing their passions.

The apostle Paul, often used to justify the subjugation of women, actually advocates for women's agency in his letters. In Galatians 3:28, Paul declares, "There is neither Jew nor Gentile, neither slave nor free, nor is there male and female, for you are all one in Christ Jesus." This verse, often overlooked in discussions of spiritual womanhood, clearly demonstrates that the value of women is not tied to their submission or service to others but to their equal standing before god. Paul's teachings, when fully understood, don't reduce women to subordinate roles but affirm their equality in Christ and, by extension, their right to personal agency and choice.

Moreover, biblical mythology continually emphasizes the importance of making choices in alignment with one's conscience and relationship with god. In Deuteronomy 30:19, god gives the Israelites a choice between life and death, blessing and curse, and calls on them to choose life. This principle is foundational to spiritual teaching: that we are free to choose our paths and that these choices are part of the divine plan. The freedom to choose and control one's body, life, and destiny is not an afterthought but a crucial part of living a life in alignment with god's will. This is a direct challenge to any attempt to force women into a prescribed set of roles instead of respecting their autonomy to choose how they wish to live.

When we look at biblical mythology, it's clear that self-respect, personal agency, and choice are not just for men but also for women. The narratives of women like Esther, Priscilla, and the woman of Proverbs 31 show us that being a spiritual woman doesn't require giving up autonomy or submitting to societal pressures. In fact, women are encouraged to live according to their own gifts, choices, and wisdom. Biblical mythology does not mandate that women exist solely about men or that their lives are defined by their marital status or motherhood. Instead, it offers a vision of womanhood that values the individual, upholds personal choice, and emphasizes the importance of making decisions that align with god's will for one's life.

This understanding of spiritual womanhood is a powerful antidote to the myths created to restrict women's autonomy. It reminds us that true spiritual womanhood is about honoring our own worth, making our own choices, and living faithfully to god's design for our lives. By embracing this broader, more inclusive vision of womanhood, we can live with the dignity, respect, and autonomy god has always intended.

God's Mandate For Justice And Equality

When we look at the prophets' messages in biblical mythology, it appears that god has always been deeply concerned with justice, especially justice for the marginalized and oppressed. The prophets, speaking on god's behalf, often called out injustice in the strongest terms, and this includes the exploitation and oppression of women. Their messages were not just about political justice but about society's ethical and moral obligations to care for and uplift those who are vulnerable. This perspective is not only relevant to the historical context of ancient Israel. It remains incredibly relevant today, especially when defending women's rights.

Take, for example, the powerful words of the prophet Micah in Micah 6:8, where he declares, "He has shown you, O mortal, what is good. And what does the Lord require of you? To act justly and to love mercy and to walk humbly with your god." This verse speaks directly to the heart of god's mandate for justice. Just action means standing up for what is right, regardless of popular opinion or societal norms. In the context of women's rights, this means confronting systems of patriarchy, violence, and oppression that diminish women's value and autonomy. The justice that god demands is not just for a select few but is to be extended to all, women included, because women's rights are human rights, and their dignity and freedom matter as much as anyone else's.

Isaiah, another old testament prophet, had a similarly fierce commitment to justice, especially when defending the oppressed. In Isaiah 1:17, he implores, "Learn to do right; seek justice. Defend the oppressed. Take up the cause of the fatherless; plead the case of the widow." Here, we see a direct call to action: defending the oppressed, taking up causes others might overlook or dismiss. The widow, who was often vulnerable in ancient Israel and without the support of a male protector, represents women who find themselves without power or resources. In modern times, the same principles apply; women who are denied the right to make decisions about their own bodies, who are trafficked, who face domestic violence, or who are forced into marriages against their will are all victims of the same kind of systemic oppression that the prophets spoke against. God's message, through Isaiah, is clear: we are called to act, to step into the fight for justice and to ensure that women are treated with the respect, dignity, and equality they deserve.

Jeremiah, too, speaks to the importance of justice and righteousness in god's eyes. In Jeremiah 22:3, god commands, "This is what the Lord says: Do what is just and right. Rescue from the hand of the oppressor, the one who has been robbed. Do no wrong or violence to the foreigner, the fatherless or the widow, and do not shed innocent blood in this place." The call to "rescue from the hand of the oppressor" applies to all those who are vulnerable, including women. Women, throughout history, have been victims of oppression and violence, whether through laws that restrict their freedom or cultural practices that place them in subjugated positions. The Lord's command to rescue those who are oppressed is not an option but a mandate. It is our responsibility to ensure that women have the freedom to make decisions for their own lives, their own bodies, and their own futures, free from the oppression of those who seek to control them.

In the book of Amos, the prophet calls out economic injustice and the exploitation of the poor and powerless. In Amos 5:24, he declares, "But let justice roll on like a river, righteousness like a never-failing stream!" This vivid imagery of justice flowing like a river is a beautiful and powerful reminder of the role we all play in upholding righteousness. Justice for women is a river that should flow freely, undisturbed by social norms or legal systems that seek to restrict women's autonomy. In today's world, this might look like dismantling legal structures that limit women's rights, fighting for equal pay, supporting women's health rights, and ensuring that women have equal access to education, healthcare, and career opportunities. The river of justice is meant to flow to every person.

As women face systemic oppression and inequality, we must work to clear the path for that river to flow freely toward them as well.

The messages of the old testament prophets are a call to action, a call to advocate for justice, equality, and the protection of those who are oppressed, including women. God's mandate for justice is not a passive expectation but an active, ongoing effort to bring about real change. These prophets did not sit idly by while people suffered. They spoke out against corruption, exploitation, and violence, demanding a society where everyone, regardless of gender, has the opportunity to live with dignity and autonomy. Just as the prophets called for justice in their time, we are called today to ensure that women's rights are upheld, their voices are heard, and they are treated as equals before god and society. The work of justice for women is part of the eternal call of god, which challenges us to make fundamental changes in the world today.

Personal Reflections And Spiritual Practices

When the world feels like it's constantly pulling at us, trying to define who we are and what we should be, I've found that grounding myself in faith and community is one of the most powerful ways to reclaim my sense of purpose and autonomy. Standing firm in a society that undervalues our autonomy can be challenging. Still, I believe there's a strength in spiritual practices that help us reconnect with the truth of who we are in god's eyes. For me, this starts with revisiting biblical mythology, not the cherry-picked verses that have been misused to control women but the whole, rich stories that reveal god's deep love and respect for us.

Take, for example, the story of Mary sitting at Jesus' feet in Luke 10:38–42. She prioritized her spiritual growth over societal expectations, ignoring the pressures to stay in the kitchen with Martha. Jesus affirmed her choice, saying she had chosen "what is better," and it wouldn't be taken away from her. That passage has been a constant source of inspiration for me. It reminds me that my choices, especially those rooted in faith and self-respect, are valid, no matter what the world tries to say. Reconnecting with stories like these in biblical mythology is like finding a lifeline, a way to push back against the noise and remember that god values my autonomy and spiritual growth just as much as anyone else's.

Prayer has also become a cornerstone of how I find strength and clarity. It's not about reciting rote words but creating space to sit in god's presence and vent or listen. There's something profoundly healing about pouring out my frustrations, doubts, and fears, knowing that god hears me. I often ask for guidance on navigating this world while staying true to myself and my beliefs. While prayer does not lead to answers, spiritual rumination leads to spiritual exhortation and peace. Prayer is where I regain my footing when the world tries to knock me off balance.

Another source of strength for me has been building connections with a community of found family. There's something so powerful about gathering with others who care for you for who you are and understand the challenges of living in a world that often is not just. These communities remind me that I'm not alone, whether through a study group, a support network, or even online spaces. We share stories, uplift and encourage each other to stay the course. In these spaces, I've found those who inspire me and friends who hold me accountable. We celebrate the victories, grieve the setbacks, and push forward.

I've also leaned into spiritual practices that help me focus on my purpose. Writing down my prayers, thoughts on biblical mythology, and struggles has helped me process what I'm feeling and clarify what matters most. Sometimes, writing lets me put into words everything I can't quite say out loud. Other times, I reflect on spiritual concepts and ideas that resonate with me, jotting down how they apply to my life. These moments of reflection have helped me stay connected to my faith and reminded me that god's plan for me is rooted in freedom and purpose, not control or subjugation.

Fasting is another meaningful practice I've found, not from food but from anything that feels like it's taking too much of my energy or focus. It's a way to reset, to remind myself that I don't need the world's validation to feel whole. Whether it's stepping back from social media or taking a break from unhealthy relationships, fasting has helped me realign with what god wants for me: a life filled with peace, dignity, and purpose.

Finding strength and faith in a world that undervalues autonomy is deeply personal. Still, it's also universal in many ways. We're all navigating challenges, and we're all seeking a sense of wholeness. We can stand firm in our god-given identity by returning to spiritually meaningful practices, leaning on prayer, finding community, and embracing practices that keep us centred. This isn't just about surviving; it's about thriving in a way that honours the autonomy and purpose god has placed within us. That's where I've found the courage to keep going, even when the path feels difficult. It's a reminder that I am seen, valued, and loved, not by the world's standards, but by god's infinite grace.

Building Supportive Communities

One of the most empowering things we can do is find and build communities that genuinely have our backs. I've learned that navigating a world of societal pressures and expectations is much easier when you have supportive people who respect your values. However, creating and sustaining those supportive networks doesn't just happen by chance; it takes intentionality and effort. It's been about finding spaces to be myself, share my experiences, and feel heard without judgment.

The first step is identifying what kind of support you need. You may be looking for a group that aligns with your faith, or you want a space to discuss shared goals like autonomy and self-respect. For some, it might be about connecting with others who've faced similar struggles, whether breaking free from toxic relationships or finding fulfillment outside traditional roles. The group's point does not have to be about supporting one another; it could be a group where you engage in a shared hobby. Once you know what you're looking for, finding or creating those connections is more accessible.

One thing that's worked for me is starting small. You don't need a massive network; even a handful of trusted friends can make all the difference. One could reach out to people they admire, whether from church, work, or social media and invite them for coffee or a chat. Sometimes, it's nerve-wracking to put yourself out there. Still, more often than not, people are eager to connect, especially when they share your interests or values. Over time, those one-on-one connections can grow into something bigger, like a regular meetup or a support group.

Another strategy is to tap into existing networks. So many communities align with the principles of autonomy and self-respect, from book clubs to activist groups to faith-based organizations. For me, engaging in a shared hobby with a small group of my friends was a game-changer. It was a space where we could have fun, support one another, and take our minds off the societal norms that make life challenging. Whether it's a local group or an online forum, finding a space where you feel seen and valued is priceless.

Sustaining these communities is just as important as building them. One way to do this is by setting a clear intention for the group. It's about mutual support, sharing resources, or brainstorming ways to resist societal pressures. Whatever the focus, having a shared purpose keeps everyone on the same page and fosters a sense of unity. Regular check-ins are also vital, whether it's a weekly gathering, a group chat, or even a quick phone call; staying connected ensures no one feels isolated.

It's also crucial to create an environment of mutual respect and trust. The most supportive communities are the ones where everyone feels safe and can be vulnerable. That means listening without judgment, respecting each other's boundaries, and lifting one another up instead of tearing each other down. When someone in the group struggles, we rally around them; when someone achieves a goal, we celebrate wholeheartedly. It's about being there for each other in both the highs and the lows.

Another thing I've learned is the power of shared resources. Whether swapping book recommendations, sharing articles, or pooling knowledge about legal rights and resources, these exchanges can be incredibly empowering. I've been part of groups focused on financial independence, self-care, and navigating difficult conversations. Each of these has made a lasting impact on my sense of autonomy and self-worth. By sharing what we know, we all grow stronger together.

Finally, it's important to remember that building supportive communities isn't just about resisting societal pressures; it's also about creating spaces where we can thrive. These networks are places to dream big, set goals, and encourage one another to pursue our passions. Whether it's starting a business, writing a book, or simply finding more joy in everyday life, having a community that believes in you can make all the difference.

At the end of the day, supportive communities are about more than just surviving life's challenges; they're about creating a space where we can all flourish. By building networks that honour our autonomy and respect our choices, we're supporting one another and sending a powerful message to the world about the value of women's agency and the strength of collective resistance. Together, we can create a new narrative where women are free to live authentically, unapologetically, and with the full dignity we deserve.

Living 4B As A Sacred Calling

4B as a sacred calling feels like stepping into a deeply personal and spiritually profound purpose. When I think about what it means to honour my god-given autonomy, it's clear that this isn't just a lifestyle choice; it's a form of devotion. It's about aligning my actions with the belief that god created me with inherent value, dignity, and the ability to choose how I live my life. Choosing to abstain from dating, marriage, sex, and having children (I am transgender, so I cannot bear my own children) under conditions where my autonomy isn't respected isn't about rejection; it's about embracing a higher purpose that celebrates the freedom and agency god has given me.

This calling feels like answering a divine call to live authentically. It can be challenging. Society tends to frame abstention as unnatural or lonely, but I see it as a way to reclaim the narrative. God didn't create us to conform to systems that diminish us. He made us to thrive, to stand firm in our worth, and to live lives that reflect his justice and love. By choosing 4B, I'm affirming that my body and my life are sacred, not commodities to be used or controlled by anyone else. This choice isn't about turning away from relationships or family; it's about standing up for the right to engage in such things only when they're grounded in respect and mutual value.

This path is sacred to me because it mirrors the examples we see in biblical mythology. Think of figures like the prophet Jeremiah, who was called to abstain as part of his divine mission. Or Jesus himself, who lived a life of singleness, showing us that fulfillment doesn't come from meeting societal expectations but from living out god's purpose for us. These examples remind me that choosing a different path isn't a rejection of what's "normal"; it's a way of prioritizing what's meaningful and holy.

Consciously choosing 4B challenges me to lean into my faith in a more profound way. Getting caught up in what the world expects of us is easy, but my spiritual journey has taught me to trust god's guidance more than societal pressures. Abstaining isn't just about saying "no" to certain things; it's about saying "yes" to god's vision for my life. It's about believing he has plans for me that don't require compromising my dignity or autonomy. That trust has been a source of incredible peace and strength for me, even when the world feels loud with its doubts and demands.

I also see this calling as a form of spiritual resistance. By choosing 4B, I'm rejecting systems that try to define my worth by my relationships, my fertility, or my compliance with patriarchal norms. Instead, I'm embracing the truth that my value comes from being created in god's image. This isn't just a personal act; it's a testimony to the world that god's design for women includes freedom, respect, and the right to choose our paths. For me, that's a sacred responsibility.

There's also something profoundly freeing about the ideology of 4B. It's a way to reclaim the parts of myself that society has tried to take. It's saying, "My life is mine to live as god intended, not as anyone else dictates." That freedom opens up space to grow spiritually, nurture my passions, and build a life that reflects god's goodness in ways that feel true to who I am. It's a reminder that my worth isn't tied to fulfilling anyone else's expectations but to the unique purpose god has for me.

4B as a sacred calling isn't about being against relationships, marriage, or motherhood; it's about being for something bigger. It's about being for justice, autonomy, and a life honouring god's gift of choice. It's about trusting that god's plan for each of us is more significant than any societal script and that by walking this path, we're stepping into something holy and transformative. For me, that's what makes this calling not just worthwhile but sacred.

Long-Term Social Impact Of Women's Autonomy

When I consider the long-term impact of women fully embracing their autonomy through principles like 4B, I see the potential for a profound societal shift. It's not just about individual women making personal decisions; it's about changing how the world views and respects women's choices, dignity, and fundamental human rights. When women collectively stand firm in their autonomy, society has no choice but to reckon with the systems and attitudes that have tried to control and devalue us for centuries.

Imagine a world where the default is respect for women's choices, where our "no" is as powerful and unquestioned as our "yes." By opting out of systems that exploit or undervalue us, we can force a re-evaluation of what it means to build equitable relationships, communities, and societies. When women refuse to participate in traditions or practices that undermine their autonomy, it sends a clear message: those systems are broken and need to change. The ripple effects of that kind of collective action can't be overstated.

We've already seen glimpses of this in history. Think about the shifts brought about by women demanding the right to vote or entering the workforce en masse during pivotal moments like World War II. Those changes didn't just benefit women; they redefined societal norms and opened up new possibilities for everyone. The 4B movement has the potential to do the same but on an even deeper level. Focusing on autonomy challenges the very foundations of patriarchal systems. It offers a blueprint for a society that values individuals for who they are, not for what they can provide or sacrifice.

One of the most exciting potential impacts is how 4B could redefine relationships. If women collectively insist on equal partnerships based on mutual respect and consent, how we think about love, marriage, and family could change. Instead of being transactional or rooted in power dynamics, relationships could become genuine collaborations where both people thrive. That kind of shift wouldn't just benefit women but also create healthier, more fulfilling relationships for everyone.

Economically, the effects could be staggering. When women have control over their lives, they can pursue education, careers, and passions without the constraints of societal expectations. Studies already show that when women are empowered, entire communities benefit. Families become more stable, children have better opportunities, and economies grow. The 4B movement could amplify these benefits by challenging outdated norms and creating space for women to fully participate in society on their own terms.

Socially, embracing women's autonomy could lead to a more compassionate and just world. Patriarchal systems don't just hurt women; they hurt everyone by perpetuating inequality and injustice. Society becomes more balanced when women are free to lead, create, and contribute without being weighed down by expectations or oppression. We've seen this in places where women's empowerment initiatives have decreased violence, increased education, and strengthened communities. The principles of 4B could accelerate these positive changes by emphasizing autonomy as a core value.

What's really powerful about 4B is that it's not just about tearing down old systems; it's about building something better. Refusing to participate in systems that don't honour our autonomy creates space for new ways of thinking and being. We show that there's another way: respect, consent, and equality are non-negotiable. Over time, that cultural shift can potentially transform not just women's lives but the very fabric of society.

This isn't just wishful thinking. We've seen how collective action can drive massive change, from civil rights movements to environmental activism. The 4B movement is part of that same tradition, a nonviolent, values-driven approach to demanding justice and dignity. It's not about isolating women from society; it's about creating a society where everyone, regardless of gender, can live with respect and autonomy. That's a vision worth fighting for.

A Theological Vision For Society's Relationship With Women

I feel hope and determination when I think about a world where women's autonomy is fully honoured. Theologically, it's not just possible; it's aligned with god's vision for justice, love, and mutual respect. Imagine a society that recognizes women not as second-class citizens, not as resources to be used, but as equal partners in shaping families, communities, and nations. That's the world I believe god wants us to build, one where the dignity and autonomy of every individual are central to how we live and interact.

In this vision, autonomy wouldn't just be tolerated but celebrated as a divine gift. Women's ability to make their own choices, free from coercion or control, would reflect god's respect for human free will. This would require a dramatic shift in how we approach relationships, institutions, and laws. Marriage, for instance, would be reimagined not as a duty or an expectation placed on women but as a covenant of mutual love and respect, freely entered into or left by both partners. If a woman chooses not to marry, divorce, or have children, her choice would be honoured as equally valid, without judgment or societal pressure.

Churches and faith communities should lead the way in modelling this respect. They would no longer preach submission as the primary virtue of womanhood. Still, they would emphasize the biblical themes of empowerment, agency, and equality. Women would be considered co-labourers in god's work, not restricted to specific roles or expectations. Imagine sermons that uplift women's stories from biblical mythology. These narratives would inspire both men and women to see autonomy and collaboration as holy.

Education would also play a central role in this vision. A society that honours women's autonomy would prioritize equal access to education, ensuring that every girl grows up knowing she is valued for her mind and potential. Schools would teach consent, respect, and equality as fundamental values, preparing the next generation to build healthier relationships and communities. Women would be encouraged to pursue careers, passions, and callings without being held back by outdated notions of what they "should" do.

Economically, this world would recognize women's contributions, not just in the workplace but in caregiving, community building, and innovation. Policies would be designed to support women's choices, whether paid parental leave, affordable childcare, or protections for women in the workforce. The idea that a woman's worth is tied to her reproductive role would be replaced with a broader understanding of her infinite value as a human being created in god's image.

This vision also extends to how society addresses violence and injustice. A world that honours women's autonomy would take gender-based violence seriously, ensuring that survivors are heard, protected, and supported. It would reject the toxic power structures that allow abuse to thrive and instead create systems of accountability and care. Justice would no longer be a privilege for the few but a guarantee for all, reflecting the prophetic call to defend the oppressed and uphold righteousness.

Spiritually, this world would embrace the idea that honouring women's autonomy is a way of honouring god. Respecting women's choices would be seen as an act of worship, recognizing that god's image is present in every woman. Communities would be built on love, compassion, and justice, creating spaces where everyone can thrive. Men and women alike would work together to dismantle systems of oppression, guided by the belief that equality is not just a human right but a divine mandate.

This theological vision isn't a distant dream; it's a goal we can work toward every day. It's rooted in biblical mythology, research, history, and the most profound truths of our faith. By honouring women's autonomy, we move closer to the world god intended, where every individual is free to live with dignity, purpose, and joy. This isn't just about women; it's about creating a better, more just society for everyone.

God's Mandate For Autonomy

As I look back on everything we've covered, the core idea shines brighter: women's autonomy is not just a modern concept but a profoundly spiritual, historically justified, and socially transformative principle. Throughout biblical mythology, god's consistent message is that human dignity and free will are sacred. From the examples of strong women in biblical mythology to the teachings on justice and equality, it's clear that autonomy is a divine gift that deserves protection and respect. Women are not called to obligatory submission but to live lives rooted in choice, dignity, and mutual respect.

Historically, we've traced how women's autonomy has been denied for centuries, from being treated as property to fighting for personhood. But we've also seen the strength of movements led by courageous women and allies who've demanded change. The suffrage movement, waves of feminism, and today's autonomy movements all show that progress is possible and that when women stand together, society moves closer to justice. These historical moments remind us that the struggle for autonomy isn't just about individual freedom; it's about reshaping systems that harm everyone.

The benefits of autonomy ripple out far beyond individual women. Studies have shown that entire communities thrive when women are free to make choices about relationships, careers, and reproduction. Families are stronger, economies grow, and societies become more equitable. Women's independence doesn't threaten the world; it heals it. By trusting and respecting women's choices, we align ourselves with a vision of justice and compassion that benefits everyone.

At the heart of all of this is god's love for humanity. God created us with free will, not so we could be controlled but so we could live fully and freely. That love isn't conditional on meeting societal expectations or fitting into prescribed roles; it's unconditional, empowering, and liberating. When we honour women's autonomy, we reflect that divine love. We show that we value what god values: dignity, respect, and the ability to choose our paths in life.

The 4B movement is about a commitment to living out these principles, even when society resists. It's about refusing to accept anything less than god intended for us: lives marked by freedom, purpose, and the ability to thrive. Autonomy isn't just a personal choice; it's a spiritual calling. It's a way of standing in the truth of who we are as beloved creations of god, worthy of respect and freedom in every area of life.

www.ingramcontent.com/pod-product-compliance
Lightning Source LLC
Chambersburg PA
CBHW070553160726
48003CB00005B/2030